LUO

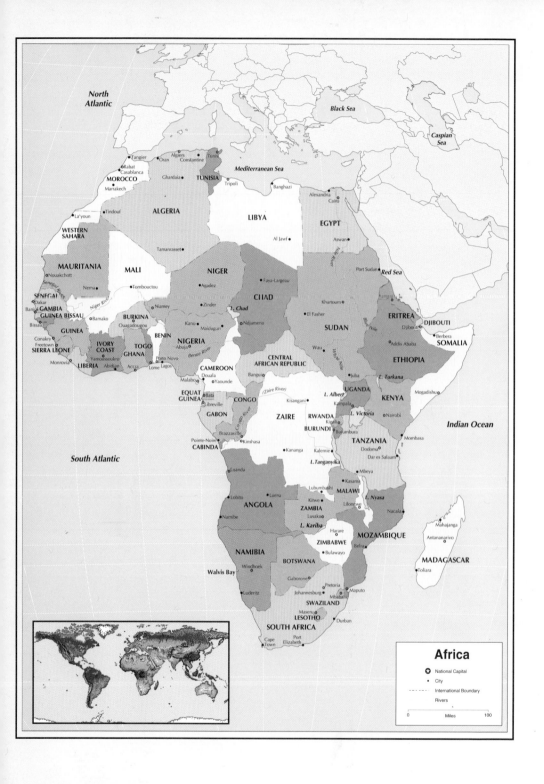

North
Atlantic

Black Sea

Caspian
Sea

Tangier
Algiers
Constantine
Tunis
Oran
TUNISIA
Rabat
Casablanca
MOROCCO
Ghardaia
Tripoli
Mediterranean Sea
Marrakech
Banghazi
Alexandria
Cairo

La'youn
Tindouf
ALGERIA
LIBYA
EGYPT
WESTERN
SAHARA
Tamanrasset
Al Jawf
Aswan

MAURITANIA
MALI
NIGER
Faya-Largeau
Port Sudan
Red Sea
Nouakchott
Nema
Tombouctou
Agadez
CHAD
Khartoum
ERITREA
DJIBOUTI
SENEGAL
Senegal River
Niger River
Niamey
Zinder
L. Chad
El Fasher
Djibouti
Berbera
Banjul GAMBIA
Bamako
BURKINA
Kano
Ndjamena
SOMALIA
GUINEA BISSAU
Ouagadougou
Maiduguri
SUDAN
Addis Ababa
Bissau
BENIN
Wau
ETHIOPIA
GUINEA
NIGERIA
Conakry
Freetown
IVORY
Abuja
CENTRAL
L. Turkana
SIERRA LEONE
TOGO
COAST
Benue River
AFRICAN REPUBLIC
Monrovia
GHANA
Porto Novo
CAMEROON
Juba
Yamoussoukro
Lome Lagos
Bangui
UGANDA
KENYA
LIBERIA
Abidjan
Accra
Douala
L. Albert
Mogadishu
Malabo
Yaounde
Kisangani
Kampala
EQUAT.
Bata
(Zaire River)
L. Victoria
Nairobi
GUINEA
Libreville
CONGO
RWANDA
GABON
ZAIRE
Kigali
Congo River
Kinshasa
BURUNDI
Mombasa
Brazzaville
Bujumbura
Pointe-Noire
Kananga
Kalemie
TANZANIA
CABINDA
Dodoma
Dar es Salaam
Luanda
L.Tanganyika
Mbeya
South Atlantic
Indian Ocean
Kasama
Lubumbashi
Lobito
Luena
MALAWI
L. Nyasa
ANGOLA
Kitwe
Lilongwe
Nacala
ZAMBIA
Namibe
Lusaka
Mahajanga
L. Kariba
Harare
Antananarivo
ZIMBABWE
MOZAMBIQUE
NAMIBIA
Bulawayo
Beira
BOTSWANA
MADAGASCAR
Walvis Bay
Windhoek
Toliara
Gaborone
Pretoria
Maputo
Luderitz
Johannesburg
Mbabane
SWAZILAND
Maseru
LESOTHO
Durban
SOUTH AFRICA
Cape
Town
Port
Elizabeth

Africa

⬢ National Capital

• City

--- International Boundary

   Rivers

0   Miles   100

LUO

Awuor Ayodo, Ph.D.

THE ROSEN PUBLISHING GROUP, INC.
NEW YORK

CODMAN SQUARE

APR - - 1996

4/96

1996 by The Rosen Publishing Group, Inc.
Street, New York, NY 10010

Copyright 1996 by The Rosen Publishing Group, Inc.

First Edition

Manufactured in the United States of America

Library of Congress Cataloging-in-Publication Data

Ayodo, Awuor.
    Luo / Awuor Ayodo. — 1st ed.
        p.   cm. — (The heritage library of African peoples)
    Includes bibliographical references and index.
    Summary: Discusses the history and lifestyle of a group of people occupying the coastal territory of Lake Victoria in Tanzania and Kenya.
    ISBN 0-8239-1758-4
    1. Luo (African people)—History—Juvenile literature.   2. Luo (African people)—Social life and customs—Juvenile literature.
    [1. Luo (African people)]   I. Title.   II. Series.
DT433.545.L85A95   1996
967.8′27004965—dc20   95-31656
                                                              CIP
                                                              AC

Contents

INTRODUCTION

THERE IS EVERY REASON FOR US TO KNOW
something about Africa and to understand its
past and the way of life of its peoples. Africa is a
rich continent that has for centuries provided
the world with art, culture, labor, wealth, and
natural resources. It has vast mineral deposits,
fossil fuels, and commercial crops.

But perhaps most important is the fact that
fossil evidence indicates that human beings
originated in Africa. The earliest traces of
human beings and their tools are almost two
million years old. Their descendants have
migrated throughout the world. To be human is
to be of African descent.

The experiences of the peoples who stayed in
Africa are as rich and as diverse as of those who
established themselves elsewhere. This series of
books describes their environment, their modes
of subsistence, their relationships, and their customs and beliefs. The books present the variety
of languages, histories, cultures, and religions
that are to be found on the African continent.
They demonstrate the historical linkages between
African peoples and the way contemporary Africa
has been affected by European colonial rule.

Africa is large, complex, and diverse. It en-
compasses an area of more than 11,700,000

square miles. The United States, Europe, and India could fit easily into it. The sheer size is an indication of the continent's great variety in geography, terrain, climate, flora, fauna, peoples, languages, and cultures.

Much of contemporary Africa has been shaped by European colonial rule, industrialization, urbanization, and the demands of a world economic system. For more than seventy years, large regions of Africa were ruled by Great Britain, France, Belgium, Portugal, and Spain. African peoples from various ethnic, linguistic, and cultural backgrounds were brought together to form colonial states.

For decades Africans struggled to gain their independence. It was not until after World War II that the colonial territories become independent African states. Today, almost all of Africa is ruled by Africans. Large numbers of Africans live in modern cities. Rural Africa is also being transformed, and yet its people still engage in many of their customs and beliefs.

Contemporary circumstances and natural events have not always been kind to ordinary Africans. Today, however, new popular social movements and technological innovations pose great promise for future development.

George C. Bond, Ph.D., Director
Institute of African Studies
Columbia University, New York

A Luo man wearing traditional warrior dress, including a cape and headdress of monkey fur.

chapter

1

THE LUO PEOPLE

THE REPUBLIC OF KENYA IS SITUATED IN EAST Africa straddling the equator, with a coastline on the Indian Ocean. It is a country of approximately 25 million people from 55 different ethnic groups. One of the largest of these groups is the Southern Luo (also sometimes called Kavirondo), who live mainly around the shores of Lake Victoria. The lake, known to the Luo as Lolwe, is the second-largest freshwater lake in the world and the source of the Nile River. The Luo occupy the Nyanza Province of Kenya, which is now considered by most Kenyans to be the Luo ancestral and traditional homeland.

Luoland has a varied topography of plateaus on the northern escarpment, plains, valleys, and lowlands. It is mainly grassland with good rain-

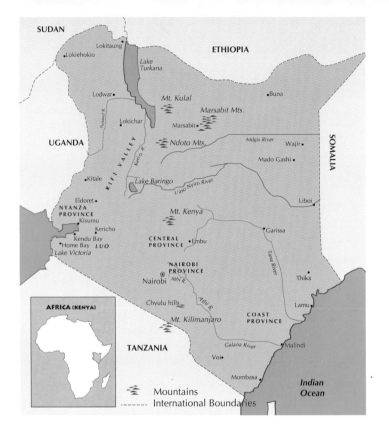

SUDAN

Lokitaung

•Lokiehokio

Lake
Turkana

ETHIOPIA

Lodwar•

Mt. Kulal

•Buna

Marsabit Mts.

Turkwel R.

Lokichar

Marsabit•

UGANDA

Kerio R.

Ndoto Mts.

Milgis River

Wajir•

SOMALIA

Mado Gashi •

•Kitale

RIFT VALLEY

Lake Baringo

Uaso Nyiro River

Eldoret •

NYANZA
PROVINCE

Liboi •

Kisumu

Mt. Kenya

Kericho

•Garissa

•Kendu Bay

CENTRAL
PROVINCE

•Embu

•Home Bay LUO

Lake Victoria

Tana River

NAIROBI
PROVINCE

Nairobi Athi R.

Thika

AFRICA (KENYA)

Chyulu hills

Athi R.

Lamu•

COAST
PROVINCE

Mt. Kilimanjaro

TANZANIA

Galana River

Malindi•

Voi•

Mombasa•

Indian
Ocean

≋ Mountains
------ International Boundaries

fall (which often floods the plains) occurring
twice a year. The long rains occur in April,
May, and June; the short rains, in August and
September. The dry season extends over the rest
of the year. Because it is on the equator, there is
no real winter season in Luoland.

About half of the four million Luo still live in
this part of western Kenya. Others are dispersed
throughout Kenya and in parts of northern and
southeastern Uganda, and some live elsewhere
in the world, continuing the migratory pattern
that originally led them to Kenya.

The Luo are a Nilotic people, a classification
based on language type and place of origin. The
term "Nilotic" refers to their origins on the

10

banks of the Nile. The other Nilotic groups are the Dinka, Nuer, Bor, and Shilluk (in the Sudan and Central African Republic); the Acoli, Padhola, Lango, and Alur (in Uganda); and the Mesarit and Daju (in Chad). Although strong linguistic similarities exist between the Luo and the other Nilotic peoples, their individual languages are distinct; a speaker from one ethnic group cannot understand a member of another group. In the same way, Spanish is classified as a Romance language but is distinct from other Romance languages such as Italian and French.

The language of the Luo, called Dholuo, is a tonal language, meaning that one word can have different meanings depending on the tone, or pitch, applied by the speaker. So, for example, the word *kendo* can mean "a stove," "marriage," or "again." Because of this tonal characteristic, it is a melodious language, and it is difficult for nonnative speakers to speak correctly even when they have mastered the vocabulary and grammar. It is written phonetically, using the Roman alphabet, and the tones of the words are understood from the context by Dholuo speakers.

The Luo arrived in the area that is now Kenya sometime between 1730 and 1760. They were then a nomadic, pastoral people who drove their herds of domestic animals (cattle being the most important) southward from the Sudan.

Rural Luo live and farm in communities of scattered homesteads close to Lake Victoria. Each family homestead has several buildings, each used for different functions.

Along the way they left behind groups of people, who settled in what is now southern Sudan and Uganda. Some later moved on into northern Tanzania. The people known as Southern Luo are those who live in Kenya and northern Tanzania.

Nine distinct Luo clans arrived in Kenya. Clans are divisions within an ethnic group according to ancestry, lineage, and the acceptance of a communal leader. They arrived in waves and over more than a century. As the clans settled in various geographical locations around Luoland, they adapted their beliefs and customs to their environment. Luo culture has subtle variations in different parts of the province. Clan identification is still important today, especially when questions of lineage arise in potential marriage matches, for example.

When they arrived at their present location, the Luo found other ethnic groups occupying the land. These were the Abaluyia, Nandi, Kipsigis, Kuria, and Kisii, not Nilotic peoples, but belonging to the Bantu and Nilo-Hamitic peoples. During a period of coexistence, the groups traded with one another, and individuals intermarried or were assimilated into each other's groups. Eventually the Luo pushed back the other groups, who today are their immediate neighbors. Periodic skirmishes occurred between the different peoples and among the Luo themselves, usually over the ownership of land, the establishment of boundaries, or the theft of cattle. However, the greatest threat to the Luo way of life occurred with the arrival of the British colonial government, which sought to control what is today Kenya.

▼ POLITICAL AND SOCIAL ORGANIZATION ▼
In the past, each Luo clan acknowledged a

A Luo clan leader, or *ruoth*, wearing traditional dress for a public celebration.

leader who earned his position by virtue of his character and leadership qualities. This ruler, or *ruoth,* and the Council of Elders upheld the laws and protected the people and their property. Land was owned by the whole community, and a piece of land that was not being cultivated could be claimed and utilized by any member of the community. Anyone who broke the laws was treated as an outcast, had some of his property taken away, or, in extreme cases, was sent into exile.

This law was modified with the arrival of British colonial rule. The British held power in Kenya from 1884—the year in which several European countries gathered together to carve up Africa for the purpose of colonizing it—until December 1963, when Kenya won its independance. The British maintained the traditional Luo leadership structure, but they chose the leaders themselves. They renamed these leaders, calling them "chiefs," and put them under the control of British colonial provincial administrators. The elders lost their official power but never ceased to occupy a position of respect within Luo communities. The British also changed the Luo system of communal ownership of land. The British divided the land into individual plots and demanded that the Luo owners have deeds proving private ownership.

The British imposed a "hut tax," which had to be paid in cash, on every dwelling. This forced people to seek wage employment in order to earn cash.

These Luo warrior headdresses combine antelope horns and feathers.

Formerly the Luo had been self-sufficient, concerned principally with providing food for their own well-being and protecting their property from aggressors by sending out their warriors. They now lost their independence and began their integration into present-day Kenya and a complex, modern, money-based economy.

Today, in addition to the chiefs mentioned (now appointed by the central Kenyan government), the Luo vote, as do all Kenyans, for the President of the Republic, for parliamentary representatives, and for members of regional and municipal councils.

The Luo produced some legendary leaders in

precolonial days, such as Gor Mahia, who was a
wise leader, a fearless warrior, and was said to
possess supernatural powers. (This is also the
name of the Luo soccer team that enjoys an
enormous following.) More recently, Jaramogi
Oginga Odinga was widely accepted as the Luo
elder and statesman. Oginga Odinga was the
first vice-president of independent Kenya and a
charismatic and politically brilliant champion of
Luo rights. Since his death in January 1994, no
successor among the Luo has emerged.

For the most part the Luo have been loyal to
the ruling political party, the Kenya African
National Union (KANU). For a long time, KANU
was the only political party. Two opposition parties have also greatly influenced the community:
the Kenya People's Union (KPU), which was led
by Oginga Odinga in the late sixties; and current-
ly the Forum for the Restoration of Democracy
in Kenya (FORD-Kenya), which was also led by
Odinga before his death. It is now led by Kijana
Wamalwa (who is not of the Luo ethnic group).

The court system, in presiding over cases of
unlawful activity, are attempting to accommodate
different views of justice. In Kenya, three acknowledged systems of law operate side by side:
customary law (or laws specific to individual
ethnic groups), common law (based on British
common law), and Islamic law (based on the
religious tenets of the Muslims), who constitute

Luo dignitaries at a formal celebration wearing braided capes of fine fabric.

about 25 percent of the population of Kenya but are less common in Luoland). If both parties to a dispute adhere to the same system of law (for example, they are both Luo, or they are both Muslim), it is settled by the officials of that system.

When parties belong to different ethnic groups and the two systems of law cannot be reconciled, the ensuing dispute is settled in the common law courts. Such was the situation in the ground-breaking case of *Otieno* vs. *Umira Kager clan*. S.M. Otieno was a Luo lawyer who married a member of the Agikuyu ethnic group. He died at the age of 55 without having left a will. His wife wished to bury him on their property close to Nairobi, where they had lived. There was an immediate reaction from the members of his clan, demanding that he be buried at his home in Luoland according to Luo tradition. Homes outside Luoland are considered by the Luo to be secondary homes in which Luo burial ceremonies cannot be performed. Such traditional burial rites are performed alongside Christian or other religious rites. The case went to court and was argued for five months, during which time the questions of the relationship between the traditional and contemporary were passionately debated. Otieno was finally buried in his ancestral land by his clan.▲

chapter

2

LUO TRADITIONS

LUO TRADITIONS, SOCIAL ORGANIZATION, AND customs have never been static. As their surroundings have changed, the people have adapted aspects of their way of life. Sometimes, such as during the period of colonial administration, change was brought about through force.

▼ CHILDREARING ▼

Elderly people have traditionally occupied a position of great respect in Luoland. Male elders constituted the governing councils, and older women undertook the education of the young, which included the transmission of cultural and social values. Thus Luo society stresses the wisdom that comes with age and experience. Nonetheless, if there can be said to be a

LUO NAMES

Luo names reflect different aspects of the society, in particular the importance of each individual birth. Thus many names simply reflect the time of day at which the birth occurred, a celebration of the moment. In general female names begin with "A" and male names with "O". In some instances a child may be named after a person of the opposite sex and so its name will not adhere to this rule. Other names will indicate the activity the mother was engaged in when she went into labor, the weather conditions, or the manner in which the infant first appeared from the birth canal. A very few names have no apparent meaning.

Female	Male	English Translation
Anyango	Onyango	Born in the early morning
Akiniyi	*	Born at dawn
Achieng	Ochieng'	Born with the sun shining
Adhiambo	Odhiambo	Born in the afternoon
Atieno	Otieno	Born at night
Awuor	Owuor	Born between midnight and dawn
Ochanda (boy or girl)		Difficult birth
Akomo	Okomo	Born during prosperous times
Akech	Okech	Born during time of famine
Ajwang	Ojwang	Born after father died
Abura	Obura	Born during a funeral
Adoyo	Odoyo	Born during the weeding season
Aoro	Ooro	Born during the dry season
Aluoch	Oluoch	Born during a heavy mist
Adero	Odero	Born near a granery
Akongo	Okongo	Born in a beer drinking establishment
Adongo	Odongo	The second born of twins
Akello	Okello	Born after twins
Akumu	Okumu	A child conceived after his mother has given birth, but before she has resumed her menstrual cycle, i.e. the birth is mysterious
Auma	Ouma	Born facing downward
Awino	Owino	Born with the umbilical cord entwined around the neck
Awiti	Owiti	Literally means a child that is thrown out—so named because the mother has had trouble giving birth to healthy babies and washes her hands of this one to avert the evil eye

* The male equivalent of Akiniyi (Okinyi) is rarely encountered but is the word for the morning.

universal principle among the Luo, it is that the most important human function is procreation. There is no question that married couples must have children, because in children lies the future of the group. Among the middle classes, smaller families are now emerging, but the majority of couples have as many children as they can. Infertility is considered a curse and is always blamed on the woman. Childless women are ignored in favor of more fertile wives, or even divorced and sent back to their parents.

Children have always been expected to be deferential toward their elders and are required to obey orders or instructions without question. These expectations have been somewhat relaxed as a result of the social upheavals resulting from urbanization and the expectation that children attend school throughout childhood and adolescence. Generally, however, children are expected to be seen and not heard. Lack of respect for authority is dealt with firmly through verbal chastisement or corporal punishment.

In relatively recent years, the first eight years of elementary education have been declared free and obligatory for all children by the Kenyan government. In reality, many children cannot attend school because their families are unable to pay for required school uniforms, supplies, and contributions toward "building funds" for the construction of schools.

Many Luo women work as traders in small markets such as this one close to Lake Victoria.

Inequality between the sexes is still prevalent. It is not uncommon for girls to be expected to wait on their brothers and male peers. Girls are oriented toward domestic duties whereas boys are encouraged to excel academically. Nonetheless, Luo women are now receiving more education and consequently entering the money economy, predominantly in clerical positions.

In families where both parents work, a domestic servant is usually employed. This servant may be an adult or a young girl who has been forced out of school by her own parents' financial situation. Women are generally employed as *ayahs* or nannies; men are more often cooks. In some families the help may be a relative. When there is no hired help, older children

23

(especially girls) are required to help with the care of younger siblings.

Today, the urban or financially able family lives in a single home. Rural Luo still build traditional family compounds consisting of several dwellings. In earlier times, children slept in their mother's house until puberty, when girls moved into a *siwindhe*, or special house presided over by a grandmother or elderly female relative. Similarly, boys had a *simba* erected for their use. Today there is still an attempt to provide separate accommodations for the sexes, but this is dependent on the space available. Children are not expected to leave their parents' home until they marry. It is the duty of the youngest son to care for elderly parents, and this used to mean that he did not move away from his parents' homestead. Nowadays arrangements vary according to the inclination and wealth of the children.

Because Luo society changes constantly, the culture and traditions that are handed down to children have also changed. In the past, for example, a Luo could be recognized by the gap left by the removal of six lower teeth between the ages of 11 and 13. This was the result of an initiation ceremony that signified entry into adulthood. This practice has died out (although the absence of lower teeth can still be seen in elderly Luos) and has not as yet been replaced by any other. The nearest equivalent has been graduation from high school. This is not surprising, as it is on reaching 18 that Kenyan youths graduate, get their driver's licenses, and become eligible to vote. These rituals today announce the onset of maturity. In urban areas, and through most of the homeland, the attitude toward following ethnic traditions is now so relaxed that it has become difficult to distinguish the beliefs and activities of Luo children from those of other ethnic groups in Kenya.

In the immediate postindependence era, some parents, particularly in urban areas, were even reluctant to teach their children the Luo language, believing that the two official languages of Kenya, Swahili and English, would better prepare their children for a national and/or international future. Education in Kenya is conducted in Swahili and English. With time, however, most Luos realized the importance of communicating in their mother tongue. Today many families speak a mixture of Dholuo, Swahili, and English.

▼ MARRIAGE ▼

As can be expected, marriage is an extremely important event in the life-cycle of the Luo people. Men are allowed to marry as many as five wives. For both men and women marriage is expected to last a lifetime, but there are occasional divorces. There are set customs related to marriage. Couples are often introduced to one another by matchmakers. That is because the lineage of a prospective mate must be keenly scrutinized. If, for example, the father of the future groom is known to practice witchcraft, or to be a habitual liar, the marriage is undesirable. However, all members of the community are expected to get married. Luo men or women who do not marry are suspected of being strange and are shunned by the rest of society.

The male members of a family are expected to marry according to age. Thus the oldest son marries first and the youngest after all his other brothers. This is because a father cannot be expected to pay several brideprices at once.

Once a couple has decided to marry, representatives of both families meet to determine the details of the marriage contract. First the prospective bridegroom, traveling with a delegation of male relatives, presents a token of his intentions, known as an *ayie*, to the woman's father through an intermediary—one of his relatives. This can be in the form of cash or livestock. The groom and his future father-in-law never actually address each other but are spoken for by representatives.

This visit is celebrated by a sumptuous meal prepared by the women, but eaten only by the men. Following this, male relatives from both sides (usually uncles) meet to decide on the brideprice, compensation to be paid by the bridegroom to the woman's family. When this has been decided upon, it can be paid all at once or in installments over the couple's entire life together. This payment represents a binding agreement between families. It acknowledges that the woman's family is losing a productive member of their household and recognizes that she is expected to remain a member of her new home. In the event of a separation, the brideprice must be repaid, but only if it has already been paid in full.

When the brideprice has been decided, the parents of the bride slaughter an ox and send the meat to several of the bridegroom's relatives. Following this, a great feast is prepared at the bride's homestead. Friends and relatives of the couple gather for a long evening of drinking, eating, and singing. After this party, the bride is entitled to go to live with her new husband.

It is only after a marriage has been tradition-ally sanctified in this way that a couple arrange a church wedding. This follows the pattern of all Christian weddings, having a ceremony in church and a reception afterward. In the period between the Luo and Christian ceremonies, the couple may decide to move in together or to await the completion of all the rites. This adher-ence to two seemingly separate, but now inter-

The various structures of a Luo homestead surround an open courtyard where much of daily life is lived. Poultry and stored produce occupy the structures that are built on stilts to avoid pests and predators.

twined, traditions recurs in many aspects of Luo, or indeed Kenyan, life.

Many rural Luo continue to live in the traditional scattered homesteads, each containing a single family group. Within each family homestead is a cluster of dwellings. In polygamous households, a separate dwelling is provided for each wife either within the family compound or, today, sometimes in another part of the town or city. The first wife occupies a position of authority and respect in relation to other wives. The women not only share a husband, but, more important, household tasks and the care and rearing of the children. In areas without running water, the trip to a water source (communal well or water faucet, river, or bore-hole) can take several hours, so a single wife's domestic duties would be overwhelming.

The majority of the Luo are now Christians and are permitted only one legal wife at any one time. Most adhere to this rule, although some men marry in the church and then take another wife under customary law. A small percentage of Luo are Muslims, and these men can marry up to four wives.

Divorce is discouraged by Luo society and by Kenyan society as a whole, but it is legal and does occur. Luo couples who are incompatible for whatever reason usually live separately or seek legal separation from the courts. Family members and the community bring much pressure on couples to resolve differences and maintain the union. The children of a union are considered to belong to the man (both among the Luo and under Kenyan law), and this discourages women from pursuing a final separation. Ironically, when men desert their families they are under no obligation to support their children. In the case of Luo Muslims, a man need only pronounce the word "*Talaka*" (I divorce you) three times to secure a divorce.

Women may divorce men only with the consent of their husband, or by paying him a set sum. In all cases divorced women are viewed negatively and face a difficult future.

The man was, and is, considered the head of the household. Certain tasks were assigned according to gender in the past. War was the province of men, as was the physical protection of the familial compound. Childrearing and cooking were entirely undertaken by women. When a home was built, the man was responsible for erecting the frame, and the woman plastered the walls. In the current economy, both men and women work outside the home, but the welfare of children and the household are still considered women's responsibilities.

Intermarriage with other ethnic groups has always occurred among the Luo, but to a small degree. Until as late as the 1950s only Luo men would marry foreigners. Foreign women would be brought into the ethnic fold and adopt Luo culture and language. Since then, however, both Luo men and women increasingly marry non-Luo partners. Because many Luo live outside the traditional homeland, the resulting marriages and offspring are more "Kenyan" in character than specifically "Luo."

▼ RELIGION ▼

As we have seen, the majority of Luo are

Christian, while a small number are Muslim. Christianity was introduced at the turn of the century by Roman Catholic, Seventh Day Adventist, and Anglican missionaries. Since then, a large number of sects have branched off from these original groups. These sects stress a particular aspect of the religion (such as the need for purity), and blend Christianity and traditional beliefs in various ways.

The Muslims are centered around Kisumu, Kendu Bay, and Homa Bay, all on the shores of Lake Victoria. This group was converted to Islam in the first half of the 1800s by Arabs who traveled up the Nile to the lake.

The arrival of Christianity and Islam have not eliminated an enduring belief and confidence in long-held traditional views. As with most Africans, the Luo have always integrated their religious sentiment into all aspects of their lives. God is not an isolated, aloof being in the sky, but an active presence on earth. There is only one God, known by various names including Nyasae (He Who Must Be Beseeched); Ruoth (King); and Jachwech (the Creator). The Luo direct prayers to the sun and the moon, but do not consider them to be gods. Rather, they are evidence of God's presence and his proximity to all creation.

There is also a belief that ancestral spirits, or the spirits of the dead, do not simply disappear when the body expires. They occupy a realm from which it is possible to help or hinder the living. They are closer to God, but removed from the living. If, for example, a person passes away under suspicious circumstances (such as abuse or murder), his angered spirit can torment the living. The spirits cease to exist only when they have been forgotten by succeeding generations. This is a gradual process, because neglected spirits can create mischief for their surviving acquaintances and family who forget them too speedily.

In opposition to God are the *jochiende*, evil spirits or devils who cause humans pain, unhappiness, and calamities. They are counteracted by God and the ancestral spirits.

Among the living, evil-minded people are also believed to exist. They are usually women and are thought to possess extraordinary powers that they employ only to hurt others. Such people are believed to be able to poison food at a glance, kill from a distance, or use various means to cast an evil spell over their adversaries. Together with evil spirits, they can be overcome by diviners who have been possessed by a superior spirit. Diviners are assisted by ancestral spirits with which they communicate through the medium of various objects they carry. Diviners should not be confused with traditional healers who cure physical and psychological ailments through the use of herbs and specially prepared tonics, as do doctors trained in Western medicine.

The Luo never built special sites of worship, but various sacred places are still revered. These include several rock formations, the most famous being Kit Mikayi (literally, the stone of the first wife), an impressive collection of large boulders stacked on top of one another. Certain trees, such as the fig tree, are also considered sacred sites in which God is present.

It is important to realize that no matter what other religious teachings they profess, almost all Luo people today accept some aspect of the traditional beliefs briefly sketched above. How this works is a complex subject, but the Luo, like many other African peoples, have found it necessary to adapt their beliefs to a changing environment that has included the introduction of Christianity and Islam. These traditions have been adopted but have not fully replaced what preceded them. They have been combined into the original system in a dynamic manner that satisfies cultural and personal expectations.

▼ DEATH ▼

Like birth and marriage, death is considered a major event and is marked by elaborate rites. The dead are buried on land belonging to the

At the funeral of a Luo chief, or *ruoth*, an ox must be sacrificed. The ox is elaborately dressed for the occasion, as is the man who guides it in the funeral procession. Here he combines Luo warrior dress with a formal tie.

deceased, not in public cemeteries. When the death has occurred outside Luoland (in Nairobi, for example, or even outside of East Africa), the body must be returned to the homeland. As can be imagined, this is an expensive undertaking and one that contributed to the formation of a Luo Union in which members of the society help each other financially when the need arises. The Luo Union was banned during a time when the Kenyan government was attempting to weaken tribal unions in order to foster national unity. This did not put an end to the social activities of the Luo community, however.

As we have seen, the family home and land belong to male progeny, and women become members of the families into which they marry.

Fathers divide their land among their sons, who will be buried on this land together with their wives and any offspring that die before their own marriages. Before his death, a man must have erected a permanent dwelling on his property. If he has not done so, burial is postponed until a house is constructed. With many Luo men working outside the homeland, this problem sometimes occurs. On the other hand, it is considered a disgrace for an adult woman to be buried on her father's land. In cases where women have returned home after a failed marriage, for example, and then died, they are buried outside their familial homestead.

Generally, two ceremonies are performed over the corpse: one religious and the other traditional. A religious ceremony (such as a church service) can be performed in any location and as many times as required (in the urban area where death has occurred, in a local church, and at the home of the deceased). The traditional rites are performed in the home. If one dies outside the home, the returning corpse enters the compound through a new entrance broken into the fence around the home, not through the front gate. This avoids the infiltration of evil spirits into the home. If death has occurred by suicide, the body is beaten to expel evil spirits before it is interred.

Funeral ceremonies (except in the case of

suicide) are elaborate events. Everyone in the
immediate community is expected to attend
and pay their last respects, as well as all those
acquainted with the deceased or with the family.
Those unable to attend the actual burial can
visit the grave when they are able, preferably
within a year. A person who ignores a death is
thought to harbor ill-feelings toward the family
and the community.

A wake can last several days and involves
singing, symbolic performances, prayers, and
feasting. The men in traditional clothing (and
this is a minority today) cover their bodies with
ashes, wear a headdress of feathers (ostrich, for
example), carry a spear and shield, and run
from one end of the compound to another
expressing their anger and symbolically battling
the evil spirits of death. All guests contribute to
the food and drink expenses. If this is not done,
the family incurs a great debt. For this reason
the scope and nature of Luo burial ceremonies
have been criticized in some quarters. Nevertheless, the expensive ceremonies continue, and
guests may have to be asked to contribute still
more in the future.

During the wake, funeralgoers vent their
sorrow by crying, shouting, and wailing. It is
considered strange not to show any emotion.
Afterward those who knew the deceased are
expected to have come to terms with their loss.

The piece of wood on top of the thatch roof of the main dwelling of a Luo homestead is called *kisusi*. It indicates that the head of the family, *pacho*, is alive; when he dies, it is broken.

Depression following this, or any other calamity, is not expected. Indeed, some say that depression does not occur at all among the Luo.

The corpse is laid to rest in the ground (often in a coffin) to the left-hand side of the door of the main dwelling on the compound (that occupied by the head of the family) if the deceased is female, and to the right-hand side if it is male.

Kenyan men frequently die without having prepared a will. This is both because it is widely believed to be an act of willing one's death, and because the customary law guides the distribution of assets when someone dies intestate (without having left a will valid under Kenyan law). However, the application of customary law to

assets acquired by someone living under
two different legal systems and engaged in the
modern economy of Kenya can lead to compli-
cated court cases challenging the distribution of
those assets. For this reason there have been
calls for revisions of the inheritance laws. A possible complication would arise if a man married
a woman under customary law and, later, a
younger wife under common law and in church.
When he died, if the younger wife appealed for
custody of his affairs under common law and in
court, she and her children would be considered
the legitimate heirs. This, of course, is unaccept-
able and unfair to the first, customary wife
and her offspring. There have been several well-
publicized cases of this nature.

Among the Luo, land and property are still
distributed only among male offspring unless
these are under age, in which case the eldest
wife manages the estate. Wives should inherit
their husband's house and any livestock he has
not distributed to his sons. This does not always
occur and accounts for the presence of older,
displaced women who formerly cared for the
young.▲

chapter

3

LUO CULTURE

TRADITIONAL LUO ORAL LITERATURE IS STILL actively enjoyed and transmitted. It includes praise songs, historical narratives, storytelling, proverbs, and riddles. Praise songs are sung to the accompaniment of a traditional Luo lyre-like instrument, called a *nyatiti*, by a professional singer who wears an anklet decorated with bells. He punctuates his songs rhythmically by stamping his foot, shaking this anklet. A praise song extols the character and accomplishments of an individual, who pays the singer for his services. Others present may also pay the singer if they enjoy the presentation.

Other musical instuments used by the Luo include the one-chord mandolin or *oruto*, and the *bu*, an enormous wind instrument made from a large gourd.

Luo musical instruments include the lyre-like *nyatiti* (above); the one-string *orutu*, played with a one-string bow (top right), and a large wind instrument called the *bu* (below right).

Historical narratives record the Luo past. They tell stories about the origin of the Luo people and clans as well as accounts of great leaders or wars. The storytelling tradition includes tales featuring both human and animal characters. The animals play a symbolic role; for example, in women's tales snakes and hyenas usually represent men. Most of the stories teach and reinforce how one can best deal with the environment and with other members of society. They also transmit Luo values and beliefs. An example of this is a story about a lame man who is ridiculed by his contemporaries but

A Luo Folktale

The Magical Girl

One evening a boy was running home to escape a heavy rain. He came across a beautiful girl who had no place to keep dry. She asked if she could go with him, and the boy was only too pleased to have her company. When they had reached his home and rested for a bit, the boy tried to kiss her. At this the girl changed in an instant into a leopard. Alarmed, the boy ran to get his parents, but when they came back with him, the girl was not to be found.

She had been hiding near the boy's house, and when the coast was clear she changed into a girl again and went wandering along the road. Soon she met another boy. As they walked together toward his home, they fell in love and made plans to be married. In the boy's home the day before their wedding, the girl suddenly changed into a rock and began to grow into a boulder. Her fiancé barely managed to escape before she filled up the entire room. He came back a minute later with his parents, but found no boulder, no rock, no girl. They never saw her again.

Little did they know that the girl had not gone far but had simply changed into a small, shiny stone. A passerby picked up the stone, took it home, and gave it to his wife. Since it was remarkably hard, she used it to roughen the surface of her grindstone. One day she went in to use the little stone, but where she had left it, a baby girl sat instead, playing with her toes. The woman and her husband brought the girl up until she caught the attention of a certain young man. This fellow accepted the parents' exorbitant brideprice demands and married her.

The newlywed woman happened to be the best singer in all Luoland. In fact, here is one of her songs:

Aloo nyar ma yawna!
Aloo nyar ma yawna!
 Koth biro ti onega;
Aloo nyar ma yawna!
Ma nadhiyo Onyango
 koni ma jajuok yidoe
 gisigalagala edipo.

Kopiago mana pande, kirik,
 kirik, acham Nyimalunga,

Apul acham Nyimalunga
 duto, ndhi ndhi sare
 ndhi.
Nyako manokwanyo noloko
 rapok pieko kendo oloko
 tawo nyalaro,

Okwero maricho, ndhi ndhi
 ndhi sare e ndhi.
Otumba nokwanyo, Otumba
 chieng nolokro hawi, ndhi
 ndhi ndhi sare e ndhi.
Oliech nokwanyo, Oliech
 chieng nolokro hawi,
 ndhi ndhi sare e ndhi.
Nengo nokwanyo, Nengo
 chieng nolokro hawi,
 ndhi ndhi sare e ndhi.

Open the door, Aloo!
Open the door, Aloo, or
 the rain will drown me!
Open the door, Aloo!
At Onyango's I saw a
 medicine-man in the
 cattle shed, whistling a
 tune,
sharpening a knife—-*kirik,*
 kirik. "I will eat the girls
 of Malunga village!

"I'm a magician and will eat
 all the girls of Malunga
 village!

"The girl who found me
 turned me into a
 grindstone, then into a
 lovely bowl
"that is sacred.

"Otumba found me and he
 will have good fortune.

"Oliech found me and he
 will have good fortune.

"Nengo found me and he
 will have good fortune."

The couple became very wealthy, as the girl had the power to get whatever she wished simply by asking for it. They had plenty of food and cattle, and never had to work. They had nothing but the best of luck in every aspect of their life.

But after they had been married for several years, the couple began to quarrel. During one of their fights the woman became extremely angry. She disappeared into thin air and never came back.

eventually—through his determination—marries the most beautiful girl in the community. This story contains three basic Luo tenets: all members of the community deserve respect; one survives by using one's wits; and all members of the community must eventually marry.

While most of these stories have a set storyline, the skilled storyteller adds details, interpretations, and dramatic emphases. Most traditional tales also contain songs, which help to tell the story, add to the entertainment of the presentation, and make the story easier to remember. In the past stories and riddles were told only at night to avoid wasting time during the daylight hours. Today they are told whenever time permits.

A contemporary branch of oral literature includes topical and political songs and formal speaking. Oratorical skills are greatly valued by the Luo, and the gifted manipulator of words is highly respected. Such skills are displayed in social, political, and religious speeches delivered in a religious setting or at any social gathering. Without a speech, a gathering of Luo people is incomplete.

New branches of Luo literature include scholarly research and creative fiction. Luo men and women professors in universities in Kenya and elsewhere now teach, research, and write about their chosen areas of study. These

LUO PROVERBS AND RIDDLES

A proverb is a short statement of fact concerning the culture (or philosophy) and the way of life of the people from which it has emerged. Here are some Luo examples.

• Kinship is kinship.
There is nothing you can do about blood ties but accept them no matter what the circumstances.
• The knives of old are double-bladed.
Old knives did not have a blunt side and thus they could cut in either direction; as do people who create discord within a family, or the community, an activity that has always existed.
• Persistence is strength.
One should never give up no matter what the odds.
• The stomach is darkness.
Usually said when children eat something suspect, this means that we do not know exactly how the stomach works, so there is no need for panic (yet!).

Riddles are short oral puzzles that challenge the intelligence of the person they are directed at. Riddles are popular with the young people among the Luo. Here are some examples.

Q: My house has no door.
A: An egg.
Q: Two legs sitting on four legs waiting for eight legs.
A: A bird on a cow waiting for a tick.
Q: My daughter who leaves hungry but returns full.
A: A waterpot.
Q: There is a sound like thunder and people run for their clubs.
A: Dinner is ready and everyone goes to the table.

scholarly writings cover such subjects
as geography, history, the social sciences, and
ethnography. Because of discrimination and traditional views about the role of women in Luo
society, female university professors are few.
Women have fared better in creative fiction, a
field in which they outnumber men by far. The
output has been small, however, because women
have little time and there are few publishers.
Luo creative literature draws heavily upon, and
is a continuation of, traditional oral literature.

▼ LUO ARTS ▼

Luo artists and craftspeople have predominantly worked with clay, wood, beads, animal
skins and feathers, and paint. Most of their work
consists of objects useful in everyday life. But
more and more of their work is intended to be
"art for art's sake," fine art to be admired simply
for its beauty and the skill with which it was
created.

Pottery, a female occupation, has always been
vital to Luo life. The vessels women make are
used for cooking (although metal pans have all
but replaced this function), storage (of food and
water and other household articles), and carry-
ing water. Without refrigeration, clay pots help
to keep perishable goods cool. Women also
weave baskets from different kinds of grass or
sisal. Sisal is a versatile medium and much em-

ployed for making rope, fashioning roofs, and—
in a now disappearing art—making skirts.

Men are the wood carvers and produce prac-
tical products such as furniture and materials for
the construction of the home (window frames
and doors, for example). In the past, men made
musical instruments such as the *nyatiti* and
drums; and round, four-legged, beaded stools.
Nowadays these particular skills are seldom
passed on to younger generations. Blacksmiths
produce hoes and other implements for tilling
the land and other metallic goods such as spear-
heads—formerly for protection, but mostly for
decorative purposes now. Luo artists today are
drawn toward the fine arts, and the community
has produced some fine painters.

Beads, hides, and feathers were traditionally
used for the creation of elaborate ceremonial
outfits—tunics, skirts, headdresses, jewelry.
Originally, seeds from plants and trees were
used for beads, but they have now been entirely
replaced by glass or plastic beads. The finery of
ceremonial attire is rarely seen now except at
funerals. The Luo today wear Western-style
clothing and jewelry.▲

A Luo boat and fisherman on the shore of Lake Victoria. Protruding from the boat are hornlike handles and an anchoring device topped with horns.

chapter

4

THE LUO TODAY

FOR MOST OF THEIR HISTORY, THE LUO
survived primarily as pastoralists. They raised
and subsisted on domestic livestock such as
cattle, and the number of cattle a person owned
was the most important factor in determining
that person's wealth and status in the community. As they settled around the lakeshore, and
especially as a result of the epidemic of
rinderpest, a cattle disease, in the 1890s, which
destroyed most of their cattle, the Luo evolved
into a predominantly agricultural community.
Also, because they lived on the shores of Lake
Victoria, fishing became a major occupation.
Today freshwater fish remain a preferred food of
the Luo. Less stress is now laid on the ownership of livestock, but it has continued to be a

significant nutritional source and also the means
of concluding marriage settlements and paying
debts.

The most common crops grown among
the Luo are different kinds of grain (such as
millet and sorghum), maize (corn), vegetables,
groundnuts (peanuts), and sweet potatoes.
These, together with fish and meat products,
form the staple foods. Diversification into other
crops such as pineapples and sugarcane has
more recently added to these staples. Agricultural plots are generally small—up to about five
acres. While 30 years ago there was ample un-
claimed land, today the increase in population
has made land scarce. Men are not generally
directly involved with agriculture. Cultivation is
usually undertaken by women and is carried
out with hand-held hoes. It is becoming more
common, however, to see the use of plows and
tractors.

Although there is some industry in Nyanza
Province (such as sugar production), this is
limited and has not provided substantial employment. Farming, fishing, and government
employment have been the major sources of
income. Since the advent of colonial rule, there
has therefore been a sizable movement of men
from Nyanza seeking work and financial oppor-
tunities elsewhere.

The migration of male labor began at the

turn of the century when the colonial government pressed Luo men into service, predominantly to work on farms settled by British subjects and to build the transnational railway. The British who settled in Kenya, known as "settlers," were given land free by the colonial authorities in the Kenyan Highlands, the most fertile land in the country, which today forms part of the Rift Valley Province to the east of Nyanza Province. The dispossessed Kenyans who had occupied this land instantly became "squatters" or "laborers." Luo men joined them as paid laborers on the settler farms.

A railroad, started in 1896 and completed in 1901, runs from the Indian Ocean port of Mombasa to Kisumu (formerly named Port Florence) on Lake Victoria, a distance of 600 miles. British authorities built it to open up trade with the populous indigenous kingdoms in Uganda. There was much resistance by the Kenyan peoples to this project. It was not meant for their use and benefit, it ran through their land, and they were required to work on it for very low wages. To secure sufficient labor, workers eventually had to be imported from abroad.

Other migrations took Kenyan Luo men to the neighboring country of Uganda in search of profitable economic ventures. Luo men began this journey as early as the late 1930s. Some settled in Uganda, never to return. In the late seventies and early eighties, the area experienced a lively and profitable Ugandan coffee smuggling trade as a result of the disorder that followed the collapse of the regime of the dictator Idi Amin in Uganda. This was accompanied by an equally vigorous smuggling trade in electronic and other consumer goods from Kenya. Yet another small segment of Luo moved farther south into northern Tanzania where there was available land and employment. They settled there under much the same conditions as the Luo of Kenya.

Today Luo men continue to work outside Luoland in large numbers in every conceivable occupation in all parts of the Kenyan Republic. They are active in government service, educa- tion, the tourist industry, food production, health services, and other fields. Many are also self-employed.

The emigration of Luo men had, and still has, an important impact on social affairs within the community. Men have always been consid- ered the heads of households, and in their ab- sence women's roles evolved to include this function. Women undertook to maintain familial stability while men became more involved in the national economy.

Today, without colonial restrictions, when a man moves to another area or city because of job availability, he generally takes his family with him. In certain cases he is unable to provide

A Luo elder smoking her clay pipe. She wears a patterned apron of skin, valuable trade-bead necklaces, and a headband with cowries.

adequate housing for his family, or he cannot leave his familial land untended. Under these circumstances, his family will remain in Nyanza Province. Despite the increased mobility of recent years, Luo have very strong ties to their homeland.

▼ THE ROLE OF WOMEN ▼

The Luo are patriarchal; hence, social and political power have typically been held by men. This is changing, and in the last 20 years the largest town in Luoland—Kisumu—has elected a woman mayor. In quick succession the voters of Karachuonyo district in Luoland elected a woman Member of Parliament (the equivalent of a member of the United States House of Representatives).

Women in Luo society have always been a part of the workforce, with clearly defined roles in the community. For about fifty percent of women this job description has remained the same, while for the other half it has changed considerably. For the former this work consists mainly of tending the crops, running and maintaining the homestead, childrearing, marketing their products in local markets, and producing salable handicrafts such as baskets. For the latter half, employment is found across the economic and social spectrum, as is the case for men, and ranges from salaried housework and

Rural Luo women run their households and take care of their children. Many Luo husbands are migrant workers working far from their villages, so their wives take full responsibility for the daily running of the household and fields. Many Luo today live and work in cities in Kenya and elsewhere.

secretarial work, to the professions (lawyers, doctors, etc.), representatives of government and international organizations, and self-employment within the business community.▲

CONCLUSION

IN RECENT YEARS THERE HAS BEEN A MARKED increase in the Luo population. This may be seen as good or bad. It is reassuring that the group is expanding thanks to improved medical attention and a decline in child mortality. There is, however, reason for concern as the growing population puts pressure on land availability, employment fails to keep pace with the population, and services such as electricity, education, and medicine fall behind the needs of the people. Many believe there is therefore a need for more industry, increased government aid to the area, and a reduction in the rate of population growth.

Nevertheless, the Luo ethnic group forms a vital and productive segment of Kenyan society.

This Luo horn player's headdress is composed of antelope horns, warthog tusks, cowrie shells, and fur.

Together with other Kenyans of his generation, this Luo boy represents faith in a future that harmonizes tradition and social change.

As we have seen, Luo culture is vibrant and constantly undergoing change to accommodate the evolving circumstances under which Luo people live. Certain aspects of the culture have resisted change, and only when they cease to serve the needs of the people will they pass away. The culture, or philosophical outlook on life, is the basis for the Luo person's worldview. Without a cultural base, the individual is adrift in a challenging and hostile world. Up to the present time Luo society has successfully remained distinct. There is no reason to believe that this will change.▲

Glossary

ayie Payment of cash or livestock given by a
man to the father of his prospective bride.
chastisement Punishment as by whipping; severe
scolding.
corporal punishment Punishment by inflicting
bodily harm.
domestic servant Person who is paid for doing
work about a home.
indigenous Native to a region or environment.
interred Buried under the earth.
jochiende Evil spirits who prey on humanity.
money-based economy System using exchange of
currency rather than goods or services.
Nilotic A group of related peoples in East
Africa, near the source of the Nile River, who
speak similar but distinct languages.
nyatiti Traditional Luo musical instrument.
oratorial Having to do with public speaking
polygamy Practice of having more than one wife.
progeny Offspring; children.
rinderpest Usually fatal virus disease affecting
cattle and sheep.

Roman alphabet (also called Latin alphabet)
 System of writing used by most western European languages and many others, including
 English.
Ruoth "King," one of several names for the
 Luo God. A clan leader is also called a *ruoth*.
sanctified Holy; set apart for religious purposes.
simba House in each homestead compound in
 which Luo boys live after puberty.
siwindhe House in each homestead compound
 in which Luo girls live after puberty.
skirmishes Minor fights in a larger conflict.
static Stationary; fixed in one place.
urbanization Process of becoming a city, or like a
 city.

For Further Reading

Amin, Mohamed; Willetts, Duncan; and Tetley, Brian. *Journey Through Kenya*. London: Bodley Head, 1982.

Amin, Mohamed, and Moll, Peter. *Portraits of Africa*. London: Harvill Press, 1983.

Dupre, Carole E. *The Luo of Kenya: An Annotated Bibliography*. Washington, D.C.: Institute for Cross-Cultural Research, 1968.

Hauge, Hans-Egil. *Luo Religion and Folklore*. Oslo: Universitatetsforlaget, 1974.

Ochieng', William R. *An Outline History of Nyanza Up to 1914*. Nairobi: East African Literature Bureau, 1974.

Oginga Odinga, Jaramogi. *Not Yet Uhuru: An Autobiography*. New York: Hill and Wang, 1967.

Ogot, Bethwell A. *History of the Southern Luo*. Nairobi: East African Publishing House, 1967.

Ominde, Simeon H. *The Luo Girl from Infancy to Marriage*. Nairobi: Kenya Literature Bureau, 1952.

Onyango-Ogutu, B., and Roscoe, A. A. *Keep My Words: Luo Oral Literature*. Nairobi: Heinemann Kenya, 1974.

Sytek, William. *Luo of Kenya*. New Haven: Human Relations Area Files, Inc., 1972.

Index

ABOUT THE AUTHOR

Awuor Ayodo graduated with a Ph.D. in Comparative Literature from the University of Illinois at Urbana-Champaign. Her specialization is African literatures in English, French, Swahili, and Dholuo as well as African diaspora literature in English, French, and Spanish.

COMMISSIONING EDITOR: Chukwuma Azuonye, Ph. D.
CONSULTING EDITOR: Gary Van Wyk, Ph.D.
PHOTO CREDITS: CFM, Nairobi
DESIGN: Kim Sonsky